# THIS BOOK BELONGS

_____

THIS HOUSE PLANNER WILL HELP YOU STAY ORGANIZED, AND KEEP ALL OF YOUR IMPORTANT INFORMATION IN ONE PLACE

IN THIS BOOK THERE ARE PAGES FOR FILLING OUT HOME DETAILS LIKE;

- YEAR HOUSE WAS BUILT
- PURCHASE DATE & PRICE
- ADDRESS
- MORTGAGE PROVIDER
- MAJOR APPLIANCES EG; OVEN, SERIAL NO, WARRANTY, PRICE
- HOUSEHOLD BILLS

EACH ROOM HAS 6 SECTIONS FOR YOU TO FILL OUT, INCLUDING;

- **INTERIOR DESIGN** - DIMENSIONS, INPUT IDEAS FOR FLOORING, CEILING, WALLS, TRIM, DOORS
- **LAYOUT PLAN** - DOTTED PAGE SO YOU CAN SKETCH YOUR IDEAL LAYOUT AND FLOOR PLAN
- **TO DO LIST** - INPUT TASKS YOU NEED TO DO FOR EACH ROOM, EG; CALL PLUMBER TO INSTALL KITCHEN TAP ETC
- **QUOTE PAGE** - INPUT WHAT JOB YOU NEED DONE, THE COMPANY, PRICE AND THOUGHTS ABOUT THEM
- **ITEMS PURCHASED** - ITEMS YOU HAVE BOUGHT FOR EACH ROOM, KEEP TABS ON YOUR BUDGET

# ORDER OF CONTENTS

HOME DETAILS

HOUSEHOLD BILLS

MAJOR APPLIANCES

KITCHEN

LIVING ROOM

DINING ROOM

MASTER BEDROOM

BEDROOM 2

BEDROOM 3

BEDROOM 4

BEDROOM 5

BATHROOM 1

BATHROOM 2

BATHROOM 3

BATHROOM 4

ENTRANCE / HALLWAY

GARDEN

CUSTOM ROOMS

# HOME DETAILS

| ADDRESS | |
|---|---|
| | |
| | |
| YEAR HOUSE WAS BUILT | |
| PURCHASE DATE | |
| PURCHASE PRICE | |
| MORTGAGE PROVIDER | |
| OTHER DETAILS | |
| | |
| | |
| | |

# HOUSEHOLD BILLS

COST PER MONTH

| BILL | PROVIDER | YEAR 1 | YEAR 2 | YEAR 3 |
|------|----------|--------|--------|--------|
|      |          |        |        |        |
|      |          |        |        |        |
|      |          |        |        |        |
|      |          |        |        |        |
|      |          |        |        |        |
|      |          |        |        |        |
|      |          |        |        |        |
|      |          |        |        |        |
|      |          |        |        |        |
|      |          |        |        |        |
|      |          |        |        |        |
|      |          |        |        |        |
|      |          |        |        |        |

# MAJOR APPLIANCES

|  | ON MOVING IN |
|---|---|
| BRAND |  |
| SUPPLIED BY |  |
| DATE PURCHASED |  |
| COST |  |
| MODEL / SERIAL |  |
| WARRANTY |  |
| DIMENSIONS |  |
|  | REPLACEMENT |
| BRAND |  |
| SUPPLIED BY |  |
| DATE PURCHASED |  |
| COST |  |
| MODEL / SERIAL |  |
| WARRANTY |  |
| DIMENSIONS |  |

# MAJOR APPLIANCES

|  | ON MOVING IN |
|---|---|
| BRAND | |
| SUPPLIED BY | |
| DATE PURCHASED | |
| COST | |
| MODEL / SERIAL | |
| WARRANTY | |
| DIMENSIONS | |
|  | REPLACEMENT |
| BRAND | |
| SUPPLIED BY | |
| DATE PURCHASED | |
| COST | |
| MODEL / SERIAL | |
| WARRANTY | |
| DIMENSIONS | |

# MAJOR APPLIANCES

|  | ON MOVING IN |
|---|---|
| BRAND |  |
| SUPPLIED BY |  |
| DATE PURCHASED |  |
| COST |  |
| MODEL / SERIAL |  |
| WARRANTY |  |
| DIMENSIONS |  |
|  | REPLACEMENT |
| BRAND |  |
| SUPPLIED BY |  |
| DATE PURCHASED |  |
| COST |  |
| MODEL / SERIAL |  |
| WARRANTY |  |
| DIMENSIONS |  |

# MAJOR APPLIANCES

|  | ON MOVING IN |
|---|---|
| BRAND |  |
| SUPPLIED BY |  |
| DATE PURCHASED |  |
| COST |  |
| MODEL / SERIAL |  |
| WARRANTY |  |
| DIMENSIONS |  |
|  | REPLACEMENT |
| BRAND |  |
| SUPPLIED BY |  |
| DATE PURCHASED |  |
| COST |  |
| MODEL / SERIAL |  |
| WARRANTY |  |
| DIMENSIONS |  |

# MAJOR APPLIANCES

|  | ON MOVING IN |
|---|---|
| BRAND | |
| SUPPLIED BY | |
| DATE PURCHASED | |
| COST | |
| MODEL / SERIAL | |
| WARRANTY | |
| DIMENSIONS | |
|  | REPLACEMENT |
| BRAND | |
| SUPPLIED BY | |
| DATE PURCHASED | |
| COST | |
| MODEL / SERIAL | |
| WARRANTY | |
| DIMENSIONS | |

# MAJOR APPLIANCES

|  | ON MOVING IN |
|---|---|
| BRAND | |
| SUPPLIED BY | |
| DATE PURCHASED | |
| COST | |
| MODEL / SERIAL | |
| WARRANTY | |
| DIMENSIONS | |
|  | REPLACEMENT |
| BRAND | |
| SUPPLIED BY | |
| DATE PURCHASED | |
| COST | |
| MODEL / SERIAL | |
| WARRANTY | |
| DIMENSIONS | |

# MAJOR APPLIANCES

|  | ON MOVING IN |
|---|---|
| BRAND |  |
| SUPPLIED BY |  |
| DATE PURCHASED |  |
| COST |  |
| MODEL / SERIAL |  |
| WARRANTY |  |
| DIMENSIONS |  |
|  | REPLACEMENT |
| BRAND |  |
| SUPPLIED BY |  |
| DATE PURCHASED |  |
| COST |  |
| MODEL / SERIAL |  |
| WARRANTY |  |
| DIMENSIONS |  |

# INTERIOR DESIGN PLAN

## KITCHEN

DIMENSIONS  _____

# OF WINDOWS  _____    # OF DOORS  _____

WINDOW 1 SIZE  _____    DOOR 1  _____

WINDOW 2 SIZE  _____    DOOR 2  _____

WINDOW 3 SIZE  _____    DOOR 3  _____

COLOR / STYLE  _____

    WALLS  _____

    FLOOR  _____

    CEILING  _____

    TRIM  _____

    DOORS  _____

NOTES / IDEAS

# KITCHEN LAYOUT PLAN

# KITCHEN TO DO LIST

| TASK | FINISHED |
|------|----------|
|      |          |
|      |          |
|      |          |
|      |          |
|      |          |
|      |          |
|      |          |
|      |          |
|      |          |
|      |          |
|      |          |
|      |          |
|      |          |
|      |          |

# KITCHEN QUOTES

| DATE | COMPANY | SERVICE/JOB | PRICE | THOUGHTS |
|------|---------|-------------|-------|----------|
|      |         |             |       |          |
|      |         |             |       |          |
|      |         |             |       |          |
|      |         |             |       |          |
|      |         |             |       |          |
|      |         |             |       |          |
|      |         |             |       |          |
|      |         |             |       |          |
|      |         |             |       |          |
|      |         |             |       |          |
|      |         |             |       |          |
|      |         |             |       |          |
|      |         |             |       |          |
|      |         |             |       |          |
|      |         |             |       |          |

# PURCHASED KITCHEN ITEMS

| ITEM | SUPPLIER | COST |
|------|----------|------|
|  |  |  |
|  |  |  |
|  |  |  |
|  |  |  |
|  |  |  |
|  |  |  |
|  |  |  |
|  |  |  |
|  |  |  |
|  |  |  |
|  |  |  |
|  |  |  |
|  |  |  |
|  | TOTAL |  |

# NOTES

# INTERIOR DESIGN PLAN

## LIVING ROOM

DIMENSIONS  _____

# OF WINDOWS  _____  # OF DOORS  _____

WINDOW 1 SIZE  _____  DOOR 1  _____

WINDOW 2 SIZE  _____  DOOR 2  _____

WINDOW 3 SIZE  _____  DOOR 3  _____

COLOR / STYLE  _____

   WALLS  _____

   FLOOR  _____

   CEILING  _____

   TRIM  _____

   DOORS  _____

NOTES / IDEAS

# LIVING ROOM PLAN

# LIVING ROOM TO DO LIST

| TASK | FINISHED |
|------|----------|
|      |          |
|      |          |
|      |          |
|      |          |
|      |          |
|      |          |
|      |          |
|      |          |
|      |          |
|      |          |
|      |          |
|      |          |
|      |          |
|      |          |

# LIVING ROOM QUOTES

| DATE | COMPANY | SERVICE/JOB | PRICE | THOUGHTS |
|------|---------|-------------|-------|----------|
|      |         |             |       |          |
|      |         |             |       |          |
|      |         |             |       |          |
|      |         |             |       |          |
|      |         |             |       |          |
|      |         |             |       |          |
|      |         |             |       |          |
|      |         |             |       |          |
|      |         |             |       |          |
|      |         |             |       |          |
|      |         |             |       |          |
|      |         |             |       |          |
|      |         |             |       |          |
|      |         |             |       |          |
|      |         |             |       |          |

# PURCHASED LIVING ROOM ITEMS

| ITEM | SUPPLIER | COST |
|---|---|---|
|  |  |  |
|  |  |  |
|  |  |  |
|  |  |  |
|  |  |  |
|  |  |  |
|  |  |  |
|  |  |  |
|  |  |  |
|  |  |  |
|  |  |  |
|  |  |  |
|  |  |  |
|  | TOTAL |  |

# NOTES

# INTERIOR DESIGN PLAN
## DINING ROOM

DIMENSIONS _____

# OF WINDOWS _____  # OF DOORS _____

WINDOW 1 SIZE _____  DOOR 1 _____

WINDOW 2 SIZE _____  DOOR 2 _____

WINDOW 3 SIZE _____  DOOR 3 _____

COLOR / STYLE _____

   WALLS _____

   FLOOR _____

   CEILING _____

   TRIM _____

   DOORS _____

NOTES / IDEAS

# DINING ROOM PLAN

# DINING ROOM TO DO LIST

| TASK | FINISHED |
|------|----------|
|      |          |
|      |          |
|      |          |
|      |          |
|      |          |
|      |          |
|      |          |
|      |          |
|      |          |
|      |          |
|      |          |
|      |          |
|      |          |
|      |          |

# DINING ROOM QUOTES

| DATE | COMPANY | SERVICE/JOB | PRICE | THOUGHTS |
|------|---------|-------------|-------|----------|
|      |         |             |       |          |
|      |         |             |       |          |
|      |         |             |       |          |
|      |         |             |       |          |
|      |         |             |       |          |
|      |         |             |       |          |
|      |         |             |       |          |
|      |         |             |       |          |
|      |         |             |       |          |
|      |         |             |       |          |
|      |         |             |       |          |
|      |         |             |       |          |
|      |         |             |       |          |
|      |         |             |       |          |

# PURCHASED DINING ROOM ITEMS

| ITEM | SUPPLIER | COST |
|------|----------|------|
|      |          |      |
|      |          |      |
|      |          |      |
|      |          |      |
|      |          |      |
|      |          |      |
|      |          |      |
|      |          |      |
|      |          |      |
|      |          |      |
|      |          |      |
|      |          |      |
|      |          |      |
|      | TOTAL    |      |

# NOTES

# INTERIOR DESIGN PLAN
## MASTER BEDROOM

DIMENSIONS  _____

# OF WINDOWS  _____    # OF DOORS  _____

WINDOW 1 SIZE  _____    DOOR 1  _____

WINDOW 2 SIZE  _____    DOOR 2  _____

WINDOW 3 SIZE  _____    DOOR 3  _____

COLOR / STYLE  _____

   WALLS  _____

   FLOOR  _____

   CEILING  _____

   TRIM  _____

   DOORS  _____

NOTES / IDEAS

# MASTER BEDROOM PLAN

# MASTER BEDROOM TO DO LIST

| TASK | FINISHED |
|------|----------|
|  |  |
|  |  |
|  |  |
|  |  |
|  |  |
|  |  |
|  |  |
|  |  |
|  |  |
|  |  |
|  |  |
|  |  |
|  |  |
|  |  |

# MASTER BEDROOM QUOTES

| DATE | COMPANY | SERVICE/JOB | PRICE | THOUGHTS |
|------|---------|-------------|-------|----------|
|      |         |             |       |          |
|      |         |             |       |          |
|      |         |             |       |          |
|      |         |             |       |          |
|      |         |             |       |          |
|      |         |             |       |          |
|      |         |             |       |          |
|      |         |             |       |          |
|      |         |             |       |          |
|      |         |             |       |          |
|      |         |             |       |          |
|      |         |             |       |          |
|      |         |             |       |          |
|      |         |             |       |          |

# PURCHASED MASTER BEDROOM ITEMS

| ITEM | SUPPLIER | COST |
|------|----------|------|
|      |          |      |
|      |          |      |
|      |          |      |
|      |          |      |
|      |          |      |
|      |          |      |
|      |          |      |
|      |          |      |
|      |          |      |
|      |          |      |
|      |          |      |
|      |          |      |
|      |          |      |
|      | TOTAL    |      |

# NOTES

# INTERIOR DESIGN PLAN
## BEDROOM 2

DIMENSIONS _____

# OF WINDOWS _____ # OF DOORS _____

WINDOW 1 SIZE _____ DOOR 1 _____

WINDOW 2 SIZE _____ DOOR 2 _____

WINDOW 3 SIZE _____ DOOR 3 _____

COLOR / STYLE _____

    WALLS _____

    FLOOR _____

    CEILING _____

    TRIM _____

    DOORS _____

NOTES / IDEAS

# BEDROOM 2 PLAN

# BEDROOM 2 TO DO LIST

| TASK | FINISHED |
|------|----------|
|      |          |
|      |          |
|      |          |
|      |          |
|      |          |
|      |          |
|      |          |
|      |          |
|      |          |
|      |          |
|      |          |
|      |          |
|      |          |
|      |          |

# BEDROOM 2 QUOTES

| DATE | COMPANY | SERVICE/JOB | PRICE | THOUGHTS |
|------|---------|-------------|-------|----------|
|      |         |             |       |          |
|      |         |             |       |          |
|      |         |             |       |          |
|      |         |             |       |          |
|      |         |             |       |          |
|      |         |             |       |          |
|      |         |             |       |          |
|      |         |             |       |          |
|      |         |             |       |          |
|      |         |             |       |          |
|      |         |             |       |          |
|      |         |             |       |          |
|      |         |             |       |          |
|      |         |             |       |          |
|      |         |             |       |          |

# PURCHASED BEDROOM 2 ITEMS

| ITEM | SUPPLIER | COST |
|------|----------|------|
|  |  |  |
|  |  |  |
|  |  |  |
|  |  |  |
|  |  |  |
|  |  |  |
|  |  |  |
|  |  |  |
|  |  |  |
|  |  |  |
|  |  |  |
|  |  |  |
|  |  |  |
|  | TOTAL |  |

# NOTES

# INTERIOR DESIGN PLAN

## BEDROOM 3

DIMENSIONS _____

# OF WINDOWS _____ # OF DOORS _____

WINDOW 1 SIZE _____ DOOR 1 _____

WINDOW 2 SIZE _____ DOOR 2 _____

WINDOW 3 SIZE _____ DOOR 3 _____

COLOR / STYLE _____

   WALLS _____

   FLOOR _____

   CEILING _____

   TRIM _____

   DOORS _____

NOTES / IDEAS

# BEDROOM 3 PLAN

# BEDROOM 3 TO DO LIST

| TASK | FINISHED |
|------|----------|
|      |          |
|      |          |
|      |          |
|      |          |
|      |          |
|      |          |
|      |          |
|      |          |
|      |          |
|      |          |
|      |          |
|      |          |
|      |          |
|      |          |

# BEDROOM 3 QUOTES

| DATE | COMPANY | SERVICE/JOB | PRICE | THOUGHTS |
|------|---------|-------------|-------|----------|
|      |         |             |       |          |
|      |         |             |       |          |
|      |         |             |       |          |
|      |         |             |       |          |
|      |         |             |       |          |
|      |         |             |       |          |
|      |         |             |       |          |
|      |         |             |       |          |
|      |         |             |       |          |
|      |         |             |       |          |
|      |         |             |       |          |
|      |         |             |       |          |
|      |         |             |       |          |
|      |         |             |       |          |
|      |         |             |       |          |

# PURCHASED BEDROOM 3 ITEMS

| ITEM | SUPPLIER | COST |
|------|----------|------|
|      |          |      |
|      |          |      |
|      |          |      |
|      |          |      |
|      |          |      |
|      |          |      |
|      |          |      |
|      |          |      |
|      |          |      |
|      |          |      |
|      |          |      |
|      |          |      |
|      |          |      |
|      | TOTAL    |      |

# NOTES

# INTERIOR DESIGN PLAN

## BEDROOM 4

DIMENSIONS  _____

# OF WINDOWS  _____  # OF DOORS  _____

WINDOW 1 SIZE  _____  DOOR 1  _____

WINDOW 2 SIZE  _____  DOOR 2  _____

WINDOW 3 SIZE  _____  DOOR 3  _____

COLOR / STYLE  _____

    WALLS  _____

    FLOOR  _____

    CEILING  _____

    TRIM  _____

    DOORS  _____

NOTES / IDEAS

# BEDROOM 4 PLAN

# BEDROOM 4 TO DO LIST

| TASK | FINISHED |
|------|----------|
|      |          |
|      |          |
|      |          |
|      |          |
|      |          |
|      |          |
|      |          |
|      |          |
|      |          |
|      |          |
|      |          |
|      |          |
|      |          |
|      |          |
|      |          |

# BEDROOM 4 QUOTES

| DATE | COMPANY | SERVICE/JOB | PRICE | THOUGHTS |
|------|---------|-------------|-------|----------|
|      |         |             |       |          |
|      |         |             |       |          |
|      |         |             |       |          |
|      |         |             |       |          |
|      |         |             |       |          |
|      |         |             |       |          |
|      |         |             |       |          |
|      |         |             |       |          |
|      |         |             |       |          |
|      |         |             |       |          |
|      |         |             |       |          |
|      |         |             |       |          |
|      |         |             |       |          |
|      |         |             |       |          |

# PURCHASED BEDROOM 4 ITEMS

| ITEM | SUPPLIER | COST |
|---|---|---|
|  |  |  |
|  |  |  |
|  |  |  |
|  |  |  |
|  |  |  |
|  |  |  |
|  |  |  |
|  |  |  |
|  |  |  |
|  |  |  |
|  |  |  |
|  |  |  |
|  |  |  |
|  | TOTAL |  |

# NOTES

# INTERIOR DESIGN PLAN

## BEDROOM 5

DIMENSIONS  _____

# OF WINDOWS  _____   # OF DOORS  _____

WINDOW 1 SIZE  _____   DOOR 1  _____

WINDOW 2 SIZE  _____   DOOR 2  _____

WINDOW 3 SIZE  _____   DOOR 3  _____

COLOR / STYLE  _____

    WALLS  _____

    FLOOR  _____

    CEILING  _____

    TRIM  _____

    DOORS  _____

NOTES / IDEAS

# BEDROOM 5 PLAN

# BEDROOM 5 TO DO LIST

| TASK | FINISHED |
|------|----------|
|      |          |
|      |          |
|      |          |
|      |          |
|      |          |
|      |          |
|      |          |
|      |          |
|      |          |
|      |          |
|      |          |
|      |          |
|      |          |
|      |          |

# BEDROOM 5 QUOTES

| DATE | COMPANY | SERVICE/JOB | PRICE | THOUGHTS |
|------|---------|-------------|-------|----------|
|      |         |             |       |          |
|      |         |             |       |          |
|      |         |             |       |          |
|      |         |             |       |          |
|      |         |             |       |          |
|      |         |             |       |          |
|      |         |             |       |          |
|      |         |             |       |          |
|      |         |             |       |          |
|      |         |             |       |          |
|      |         |             |       |          |
|      |         |             |       |          |
|      |         |             |       |          |
|      |         |             |       |          |

# PURCHASED BEDROOM 5 ITEMS

| ITEM | SUPPLIER | COST |
|---|---|---|
|  |  |  |
|  |  |  |
|  |  |  |
|  |  |  |
|  |  |  |
|  |  |  |
|  |  |  |
|  |  |  |
|  |  |  |
|  |  |  |
|  |  |  |
|  |  |  |
|  |  |  |
|  | TOTAL |  |

# NOTES

# INTERIOR DESIGN PLAN

## BATHROOM 1

DIMENSIONS  _____

# OF WINDOWS  _____  # OF DOORS  _____

WINDOW 1 SIZE  _____  DOOR 1  _____

WINDOW 2 SIZE  _____  DOOR 2  _____

WINDOW 3 SIZE  _____  DOOR 3  _____

COLOR / STYLE  _____

    WALLS  _____

    FLOOR  _____

    CEILING  _____

    TRIM  _____

    DOORS  _____

NOTES / IDEAS

# BATHROOM I PLAN

# BATHROOM I TO DO LIST

| TASK | FINISHED |
|------|----------|
|      |          |
|      |          |
|      |          |
|      |          |
|      |          |
|      |          |
|      |          |
|      |          |
|      |          |
|      |          |
|      |          |
|      |          |
|      |          |
|      |          |
|      |          |

# BATHROOM I QUOTES

| DATE | COMPANY | SERVICE/JOB | PRICE | THOUGHTS |
|------|---------|-------------|-------|----------|
|      |         |             |       |          |
|      |         |             |       |          |
|      |         |             |       |          |
|      |         |             |       |          |
|      |         |             |       |          |
|      |         |             |       |          |
|      |         |             |       |          |
|      |         |             |       |          |
|      |         |             |       |          |
|      |         |             |       |          |
|      |         |             |       |          |
|      |         |             |       |          |
|      |         |             |       |          |
|      |         |             |       |          |

# PURCHASED BATHROOM 1 ITEMS

| ITEM | SUPPLIER | COST |
|---|---|---|
|  |  |  |
|  |  |  |
|  |  |  |
|  |  |  |
|  |  |  |
|  |  |  |
|  |  |  |
|  |  |  |
|  |  |  |
|  |  |  |
|  |  |  |
|  |  |  |
|  | TOTAL |  |

# NOTES

# INTERIOR DESIGN PLAN

## BATHROOM 2

DIMENSIONS _____

# OF WINDOWS _____ # OF DOORS _____

WINDOW 1 SIZE _____ DOOR 1 _____

WINDOW 2 SIZE _____ DOOR 2 _____

WINDOW 3 SIZE _____ DOOR 3 _____

COLOR / STYLE _____

   WALLS _____

   FLOOR _____

   CEILING _____

   TRIM _____

   DOORS _____

NOTES / IDEAS

# BATHROOM 2 PLAN

# BATHROOM 2 TO DO LIST

| TASK | FINISHED |
|------|----------|
|      |          |
|      |          |
|      |          |
|      |          |
|      |          |
|      |          |
|      |          |
|      |          |
|      |          |
|      |          |
|      |          |
|      |          |
|      |          |
|      |          |

# BATHROOM 2 QUOTES

| DATE | COMPANY | SERVICE/JOB | PRICE | THOUGHTS |
|------|---------|-------------|-------|----------|
|      |         |             |       |          |
|      |         |             |       |          |
|      |         |             |       |          |
|      |         |             |       |          |
|      |         |             |       |          |
|      |         |             |       |          |
|      |         |             |       |          |
|      |         |             |       |          |
|      |         |             |       |          |
|      |         |             |       |          |
|      |         |             |       |          |
|      |         |             |       |          |
|      |         |             |       |          |
|      |         |             |       |          |
|      |         |             |       |          |

# PURCHASED BATHROOM 2 ITEMS

| ITEM | SUPPLIER | COST |
|---|---|---|
|  |  |  |
|  |  |  |
|  |  |  |
|  |  |  |
|  |  |  |
|  |  |  |
|  |  |  |
|  |  |  |
|  |  |  |
|  |  |  |
|  |  |  |
|  |  |  |
|  |  |  |
|  | TOTAL |  |

# NOTES

# INTERIOR DESIGN PLAN

## BATHROOM 3

DIMENSIONS  _____

# OF WINDOWS  _____  # OF DOORS  _____

WINDOW 1 SIZE  _____  DOOR 1  _____

WINDOW 2 SIZE  _____  DOOR 2  _____

WINDOW 3 SIZE  _____  DOOR 3  _____

COLOR / STYLE  _____

    WALLS  _____

    FLOOR  _____

    CEILING  _____

    TRIM  _____

    DOORS  _____

NOTES / IDEAS

# BATHROOM 3 PLAN

# BATHROOM 3 TO DO LIST

| TASK | FINISHED |
|------|----------|
|      |          |
|      |          |
|      |          |
|      |          |
|      |          |
|      |          |
|      |          |
|      |          |
|      |          |
|      |          |
|      |          |
|      |          |
|      |          |
|      |          |
|      |          |

# BATHROOM 3 QUOTES

| DATE | COMPANY | SERVICE/JOB | PRICE | THOUGHTS |
|------|---------|-------------|-------|----------|
|      |         |             |       |          |
|      |         |             |       |          |
|      |         |             |       |          |
|      |         |             |       |          |
|      |         |             |       |          |
|      |         |             |       |          |
|      |         |             |       |          |
|      |         |             |       |          |
|      |         |             |       |          |
|      |         |             |       |          |
|      |         |             |       |          |
|      |         |             |       |          |
|      |         |             |       |          |
|      |         |             |       |          |
|      |         |             |       |          |

# PURCHASED BATHROOM 3 ITEMS

| ITEM | SUPPLIER | COST |
|------|----------|------|
|  |  |  |
|  |  |  |
|  |  |  |
|  |  |  |
|  |  |  |
|  |  |  |
|  |  |  |
|  |  |  |
|  |  |  |
|  |  |  |
|  |  |  |
|  |  |  |
|  |  |  |
|  | TOTAL |  |

# NOTES

# INTERIOR DESIGN PLAN

## BATHROOM 4

DIMENSIONS  _____

\# OF WINDOWS  _____  # OF DOORS  _____

WINDOW 1 SIZE  _____  DOOR 1  _____

WINDOW 2 SIZE  _____  DOOR 2  _____

WINDOW 3 SIZE  _____  DOOR 3  _____

COLOR / STYLE  _____

    WALLS  _____

    FLOOR  _____

    CEILING  _____

    TRIM  _____

    DOORS  _____

NOTES / IDEAS

# BATHROOM 4 PLAN

# BATHROOM 4 TO DO LIST

| TASK | FINISHED |
|------|----------|
|      |          |
|      |          |
|      |          |
|      |          |
|      |          |
|      |          |
|      |          |
|      |          |
|      |          |
|      |          |
|      |          |
|      |          |
|      |          |
|      |          |

# BATHROOM 4 QUOTES

| DATE | COMPANY | SERVICE/JOB | PRICE | THOUGHTS |
|------|---------|-------------|-------|----------|
|      |         |             |       |          |
|      |         |             |       |          |
|      |         |             |       |          |
|      |         |             |       |          |
|      |         |             |       |          |
|      |         |             |       |          |
|      |         |             |       |          |
|      |         |             |       |          |
|      |         |             |       |          |
|      |         |             |       |          |
|      |         |             |       |          |
|      |         |             |       |          |
|      |         |             |       |          |
|      |         |             |       |          |
|      |         |             |       |          |

# PURCHASED BATHROOM 4 ITEMS

| ITEM | SUPPLIER | COST |
|---|---|---|
|  |  |  |
|  |  |  |
|  |  |  |
|  |  |  |
|  |  |  |
|  |  |  |
|  |  |  |
|  |  |  |
|  |  |  |
|  |  |  |
|  |  |  |
|  |  |  |
|  |  |  |
|  |  |  |
|  | TOTAL |  |

# NOTES

# INTERIOR DESIGN PLAN
## ENTRANCE / HALLWAY

DIMENSIONS  _____

# OF WINDOWS  _____     # OF DOORS  _____

WINDOW 1 SIZE  _____     DOOR 1  _____

WINDOW 2 SIZE  _____     DOOR 2  _____

WINDOW 3 SIZE  _____     DOOR 3  _____

COLOR / STYLE  _____

    WALLS  _____

    FLOOR  _____

    CEILING  _____

    TRIM  _____

    DOORS  _____

NOTES / IDEAS

# ENTRANCE / HALLWAY PLAN

# ENTRANCE / HALLWAY TO DO LIST

| TASK | FINISHED |
|------|----------|
|      |          |
|      |          |
|      |          |
|      |          |
|      |          |
|      |          |
|      |          |
|      |          |
|      |          |
|      |          |
|      |          |
|      |          |
|      |          |
|      |          |
|      |          |

# ENTRANCE / HALLWAY QUOTES

| DATE | COMPANY | SERVICE/JOB | PRICE | THOUGHTS |
|------|---------|-------------|-------|----------|
|      |         |             |       |          |
|      |         |             |       |          |
|      |         |             |       |          |
|      |         |             |       |          |
|      |         |             |       |          |
|      |         |             |       |          |
|      |         |             |       |          |
|      |         |             |       |          |
|      |         |             |       |          |
|      |         |             |       |          |
|      |         |             |       |          |
|      |         |             |       |          |
|      |         |             |       |          |
|      |         |             |       |          |
|      |         |             |       |          |

# PURCHASED ENTRANCE / HALLWAY ITEMS

| ITEM | SUPPLIER | COST |
|------|----------|------|
|      |          |      |
|      |          |      |
|      |          |      |
|      |          |      |
|      |          |      |
|      |          |      |
|      |          |      |
|      |          |      |
|      |          |      |
|      |          |      |
|      |          |      |
|      |          |      |
|      |          |      |
|      | TOTAL    |      |

# NOTES

# DESIGN PLAN

## GARDEN

DIMENSIONS _____

_____  _____

_____  _____

_____  _____

_____

COLOR / STYLE _____

FENCE _____

GROUND _____

LIGHTING _____

SEATING _____

DECKING _____

NOTES / IDEAS

# GARDEN PLAN

# GARDEN TO DO LIST

| TASK | FINISHED |
|------|----------|
|      |          |
|      |          |
|      |          |
|      |          |
|      |          |
|      |          |
|      |          |
|      |          |
|      |          |
|      |          |
|      |          |
|      |          |
|      |          |
|      |          |

# GARDEN QUOTES

| DATE | COMPANY | SERVICE/JOB | PRICE | THOUGHTS |
|------|---------|-------------|-------|----------|
|      |         |             |       |          |
|      |         |             |       |          |
|      |         |             |       |          |
|      |         |             |       |          |
|      |         |             |       |          |
|      |         |             |       |          |
|      |         |             |       |          |
|      |         |             |       |          |
|      |         |             |       |          |
|      |         |             |       |          |
|      |         |             |       |          |
|      |         |             |       |          |
|      |         |             |       |          |
|      |         |             |       |          |

# PURCHASED GARDEN ITEMS

| ITEM | SUPPLIER | COST |
|------|----------|------|
|  |  |  |
|  |  |  |
|  |  |  |
|  |  |  |
|  |  |  |
|  |  |  |
|  |  |  |
|  |  |  |
|  |  |  |
|  |  |  |
|  |  |  |
|  |  |  |
|  |  |  |
|  |  |  |
|  | TOTAL |  |

# NOTES

# INTERIOR DESIGN PLAN

_____

DIMENSIONS  _____

# OF WINDOWS  _____   # OF DOORS  _____

WINDOW 1 SIZE  _____   DOOR 1  _____

WINDOW 2 SIZE  _____   DOOR 2  _____

WINDOW 3 SIZE  _____   DOOR 3  _____

COLOR / STYLE  _____

   WALLS  _____

   FLOOR  _____

   CEILING  _____

   TRIM  _____

   DOORS  _____

NOTES / IDEAS

_____ PLAN

_____ TO DO LIST

| TASK | FINISHED |
|------|----------|
|  |  |
|  |  |
|  |  |
|  |  |
|  |  |
|  |  |
|  |  |
|  |  |
|  |  |
|  |  |
|  |  |
|  |  |
|  |  |
|  |  |
|  |  |
|  |  |

_____ QUOTES

| DATE | COMPANY | SERVICE/JOB | PRICE | THOUGHTS |
|------|---------|-------------|-------|----------|
|      |         |             |       |          |
|      |         |             |       |          |
|      |         |             |       |          |
|      |         |             |       |          |
|      |         |             |       |          |
|      |         |             |       |          |
|      |         |             |       |          |
|      |         |             |       |          |
|      |         |             |       |          |
|      |         |             |       |          |
|      |         |             |       |          |
|      |         |             |       |          |
|      |         |             |       |          |
|      |         |             |       |          |
|      |         |             |       |          |

# PURCHASED _____ ITEMS

| ITEM | SUPPLIER | COST |
|---|---|---|
|  |  |  |
|  |  |  |
|  |  |  |
|  |  |  |
|  |  |  |
|  |  |  |
|  |  |  |
|  |  |  |
|  |  |  |
|  |  |  |
|  |  |  |
|  |  |  |
|  |  |  |
|  |  |  |
|  | TOTAL |  |

# NOTES

# INTERIOR DESIGN PLAN

_____

DIMENSIONS  _____

# OF WINDOWS  _____  # OF DOORS  _____

WINDOW 1 SIZE  _____  DOOR 1  _____

WINDOW 2 SIZE  _____  DOOR 2  _____

WINDOW 3 SIZE  _____  DOOR 3  _____

COLOR / STYLE  _____

    WALLS  _____

    FLOOR  _____

    CEILING  _____

    TRIM  _____

    DOORS  _____

NOTES / IDEAS

_____ PLAN

_____ TO DO LIST

| TASK | FINISHED |
|------|----------|
|      |          |
|      |          |
|      |          |
|      |          |
|      |          |
|      |          |
|      |          |
|      |          |
|      |          |
|      |          |
|      |          |
|      |          |
|      |          |
|      |          |
|      |          |

# _____ QUOTES

| DATE | COMPANY | SERVICE/JOB | PRICE | THOUGHTS |
|------|---------|-------------|-------|----------|
|      |         |             |       |          |
|      |         |             |       |          |
|      |         |             |       |          |
|      |         |             |       |          |
|      |         |             |       |          |
|      |         |             |       |          |
|      |         |             |       |          |
|      |         |             |       |          |
|      |         |             |       |          |
|      |         |             |       |          |
|      |         |             |       |          |
|      |         |             |       |          |
|      |         |             |       |          |
|      |         |             |       |          |

# PURCHASED _____ ITEMS

| ITEM | SUPPLIER | COST |
|---|---|---|
|  |  |  |
|  |  |  |
|  |  |  |
|  |  |  |
|  |  |  |
|  |  |  |
|  |  |  |
|  |  |  |
|  |  |  |
|  |  |  |
|  |  |  |
|  |  |  |
|  |  |  |
|  |  |  |
|  | TOTAL |  |

# NOTES

# INTERIOR DESIGN PLAN

_____

DIMENSIONS  _____

# OF WINDOWS  _____   # OF DOORS  _____

WINDOW 1 SIZE  _____   DOOR 1  _____

WINDOW 2 SIZE  _____   DOOR 2  _____

WINDOW 3 SIZE  _____   DOOR 3  _____

COLOR / STYLE  _____

   WALLS  _____

   FLOOR  _____

   CEILING  _____

   TRIM  _____

   DOORS  _____

---

NOTES / IDEAS

_____ PLAN

_____ TO DO LIST

| TASK | FINISHED |
|------|----------|
|      |          |
|      |          |
|      |          |
|      |          |
|      |          |
|      |          |
|      |          |
|      |          |
|      |          |
|      |          |
|      |          |
|      |          |
|      |          |
|      |          |
|      |          |

# _____ QUOTES

| DATE | COMPANY | SERVICE/JOB | PRICE | THOUGHTS |
|------|---------|-------------|-------|----------|
|      |         |             |       |          |
|      |         |             |       |          |
|      |         |             |       |          |
|      |         |             |       |          |
|      |         |             |       |          |
|      |         |             |       |          |
|      |         |             |       |          |
|      |         |             |       |          |
|      |         |             |       |          |
|      |         |             |       |          |
|      |         |             |       |          |
|      |         |             |       |          |
|      |         |             |       |          |
|      |         |             |       |          |
|      |         |             |       |          |

# PURCHASED _____ ITEMS

| ITEM | SUPPLIER | COST |
|---|---|---|
|  |  |  |
|  |  |  |
|  |  |  |
|  |  |  |
|  |  |  |
|  |  |  |
|  |  |  |
|  |  |  |
|  |  |  |
|  |  |  |
|  |  |  |
|  |  |  |
|  | TOTAL |  |

# NOTES

# INTERIOR DESIGN PLAN

_____

DIMENSIONS _____

# OF WINDOWS _____ # OF DOORS _____

WINDOW 1 SIZE _____ DOOR 1 _____

WINDOW 2 SIZE _____ DOOR 2 _____

WINDOW 3 SIZE _____ DOOR 3 _____

COLOR / STYLE _____

   WALLS _____

   FLOOR _____

   CEILING _____

   TRIM _____

   DOORS _____

NOTES / IDEAS

_____ PLAN

_____ TO DO LIST

| TASK | FINISHED |
|------|----------|
|      |          |
|      |          |
|      |          |
|      |          |
|      |          |
|      |          |
|      |          |
|      |          |
|      |          |
|      |          |
|      |          |
|      |          |
|      |          |
|      |          |
|      |          |

_____ QUOTES

| DATE | COMPANY | SERVICE/JOB | PRICE | THOUGHTS |
|------|---------|-------------|-------|----------|
|      |         |             |       |          |
|      |         |             |       |          |
|      |         |             |       |          |
|      |         |             |       |          |
|      |         |             |       |          |
|      |         |             |       |          |
|      |         |             |       |          |
|      |         |             |       |          |
|      |         |             |       |          |
|      |         |             |       |          |
|      |         |             |       |          |
|      |         |             |       |          |
|      |         |             |       |          |
|      |         |             |       |          |
|      |         |             |       |          |

# PURCHASED _____ ITEMS

| ITEM | SUPPLIER | COST |
|------|----------|------|
|      |          |      |
|      |          |      |
|      |          |      |
|      |          |      |
|      |          |      |
|      |          |      |
|      |          |      |
|      |          |      |
|      |          |      |
|      |          |      |
|      |          |      |
|      |          |      |
|      |          |      |
|      |          |      |
|      | TOTAL    |      |

# NOTES

Printed in Great Britain
by Amazon